Animals on the Farm

Sue Barraclough

Raintree

Chicago, Illinois

Photo research by Ruth Blair and Kay Altwegg
Designed by Jo Hinton-Malivoire and bigtop design ltd
Printed and bound in China by South China Printing Company
10 09 08 07 06
10 9 8 7 6 5 4 3 2 1

Library of Congress Cataloging-in-Publication Data
Barraclough, Sue.
  Animals on the farm / Sue Barraclough.
     p. cm. -- (Animal worlds)
  Includes index.
  ISBN 1-4109-1899-8 (library binding - hardcover) -- ISBN 1-4109-1904-8 (pbk.)
  1. Domestic animals--Juvenile literature. I. Title. II. Series: Barraclough, Sue. Animal worlds.
  SF75.5.B37 2005
  636--dc22
                                    2005006756
Acknowledgments
The author and publisher are grateful to the following for permission to reproduce copyright
material: Agripicture p. 11; Agripicture/Peter Dean pp. 10, 16, 19, 20, 21; Alamy/D Hurst p.
22; Alamy/Robert Harding Picture Library Ltd p. 13; Ardea/Jean Michel Labat p. 14; Bruce
Coleman pp. 16, 17; Corbis p. 6; Corbis/Ariel Skelley pp. 4, 5; Corbis/Philip Gould p. 23;
FLPA/Gerard Lacz p. 7; FLPA/Heidi Hans-Juergen Koch; Minden Pictures p. 18; FLPA/Sunset p.
12; Harcourt Index p. 9; Naturepl.com/Lynn M Stone p. 8; NHPA/ p. 15; NHPA/Susanne
Danegger pp. 17, 19.

Cover photograph reproduced with permission of photolibrary.com/osf.

Some words are shown in bold, **like this**. You can find out
what they mean by looking in the glossary.

Contents

Animals on the Farm

Have you ever been to a **farm**?

Cows, sheep, and goats live on farms.

5

Different Farm Animals

Chickens are farm animals, too.

Chickens have feathers all over their bodies.

Sheep have thick woolly coats.

What is your favorite farm animal?

Barns and Fields

Farm animals live in fields and barns.

These cows have plenty of green grass to eat.

Chickens are kept in a house at night to keep them safe.

The farmer lets them out in the morning.

9

Food and Water

Farm animals need to eat food.

Peck!

Peck!

These chicks eat grain from a dish.

Farm animals need water to drink, too.

Slurp!

This cow takes a long drink.

11

Useful Animals

Farm animals give us food such as cheese and milk.

Can you think of which animal gives us eggs?

Sheep have their woolly coats cut off in the **summer**.

We can make warm clothes with the wool.

Baby Farm Animals

Baby farm animals have special names.

Baby pigs are called piglets. Baby sheep are called lambs.

Moving Around

Geese waddle from side to side as they walk.

Young lambs leap
when they play.

Horses move fast
when they run.

Making Noises

Farm animals make all kinds of noises.

Cock-a-doodle-doo!

Can you make these animal noises?

Baaa!

What is your favorite farm animal sound?

Moo!

19

Animal Health

Animals have special doctors, called **veterinarians**.

If a farm animal is sick, the veterinarian comes out to the farm.

This veterinarian gives an animal medicine to make it better.

Caring and Cleaning

There is plenty of work to do on a farm.

Farm animals need to be kept clean.

This farmer cares for his horse.

Glossary

farm place where animals are cared for by people

summer season of the year when it is warmest

veterinarian animal doctor

Index

Notes for adults

Animal Worlds investigates a variety of animals by looking at their distinguishing features and characteristics and by exploring their different environments.

This series supports a young child's knowledge and understanding of their world. The books are designed to help children extend their vocabulary as they are introduced to new words. Words are used in context in each book to enable young children to gradually incorporate them into their own vocabulary.

Follow-up activities:

Encourage children to draw and record what they have learned about farm animals. Use rhymes such as 'Old MacDonald' to explore different animal sounds.

24